ONE THOUSAND DOLLARS
AND OTHER PLAYS

Stage 2

...chard Rockwell's father is one of the richest men in New ...k. He thinks that money can buy anything you want. ...t certainly helps with most things, but can it buy love for ...oung Richard?

...bby Gillian has a different problem. His uncle left him ...ousand dollars in his will, and Bobby doesn't know what ...end it on. People think that he is only interested in girls, ...agne, and betting on horses, but perhaps there is more ... than that.

... Chandler and Miss Martha, money is less ... than love. But they both discover the sad truth ... is only too easy to say or do the wrong thing, and ...heir chance of love.

..., whose real name was William Sidney Porter (1862–1910), ...merican short-story writer, who tried a number of jobs, ... farming, book-keeping, and journalism. In 1897 he was ... guilty of stealing money from the bank where he was ... and it was in prison that he decided to become a ... Later he moved to New York, where he published over six h... lred short stories, including the popular collections *Cabbage and Kings* and *The Four Million*.

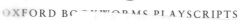

OXFORD BOOKWORMS

For a full list of titles in all the Oxford Bookworms series,
please refer to the *Oxford English* catalogue.

OXFORD BOOKWORMS PLAYSCRIPTS

Stage 1

A Ghost in Love and Other Plays *Michael Dean*

The Murder of Mary Jones *Tim Vicary*

Sherlock Holmes: Two Plays
Sir Arthur Conan Doyle
(retold by John Escott)

Stage 2

The Importance of Being Earnest
Oscar Wilde
(retold by Susan Kingsley)

Much Ado About Nothing
William Shakespeare
(retold by Alistair McCallum)

One Thousand Dollars and Other Plays
O. Henry
(retold by John Escott)

Romeo & Juliet
William Shakespeare
(retold by Alistair McCallum)

O. HENRY

One Thousand Dollars
and Other Plays

Retold by
John Escott

OXFORD UNIVERSITY PRESS
2000

OXFORD
UNIVERSITY PRESS

Great Clarendon Street, Oxford OX2 6DP

Oxford New York

Athens Auckland Bangkok Bogotá Buenos Aires Calcutta Cape Town
Chennai Dar es Salaam Delhi Florence Hong Kong Istanbul Karachi
Kuala Lumpur Madrid Melbourne Mexico City Mumbai Nairobi
Paris São Paulo Shanghai Singapore Taipei Tokyo Toronto Warsaw
and associated companies in
Berlin Ibadan

OXFORD and OXFORD ENGLISH
are trade marks of Oxford University Press
ISBN 0 19 423216 6

Illustrated by Susan Scott
Printed in Hong Kong

CONTENTS

INTRODUCTION

A young man is in love with a beautiful girl. But can his rich father's money help him to marry her?

CHARACTERS IN THE PLAY

Anthony Rockwell, a rich man
Richard Rockwell, his son
Aunt Ellen, Anthony's sister and Richard's aunt
Miss Lantry, a beautiful young woman
Taxi driver
Kelly, a man who works for Anthony Rockwell

PERFORMANCE NOTES

Scene 1: A room at Anthony Rockwell's home, with a desk and two or three chairs
Scene 2: As Scene 1
Scene 3: As Scene 1
Scene 4: The inside of a taxi, with one long seat at the back, and a single seat at the front for the driver
Scene 5: In Anthony Rockwell's bedroom, a room with a bed, a cupboard and two chairs
Scene 6: As Scene 1

You will need a book, a cup, a glass, a ring, and a packet of sheets of paper (to look like money).

All that Money can Buy

A fine boy

A room at Anthony Rockwell's house in New York. He is sitting at his desk reading. His son, Richard, comes in.

RICHARD You wanted to see me, father?

ANTHONY Richard, what do you pay for your suits?

RICHARD *(Surprised)* About sixty dollars, I think, Dad.

ANTHONY You're a fine boy. Some young men pay more than a hundred dollars. You have more money than most of them, but you're careful.

RICHARD *(Sadly)* Yes, Dad.

ANTHONY Yes, you're a fine boy, and you can thank money for that. Money will do it every time.

Richard sits down in a chair. He looks sad.

RICHARD There are some things that money can't do.

ANTHONY Now don't say that. You can buy anything.

RICHARD Your money can't buy me a way into older and better families than ours.

ANTHONY *(Angrily)* Can't it? *(Looking closely at Richard)* There's something wrong. What is it?

RICHARD Well, Dad . . .

ANTHONY Tell me. I can get ten million dollars in twenty-four hours. I can have a boat ready to take you to the Bahamas in two days. Why aren't you happy?

RICHARD   Well . . . there's a girl . . .

ANTHONY   (*Interested*) What's her name? You've got money, and you're a nice young man. Take her for a walk, or a ride. Walk home with her from church.

'Why aren't you happy?'

RICHARD You don't know her family. Every hour of her
time is planned days before. I love her, but how
can I tell her? I can't write down all the things
that I want to say.

ANTHONY Are you telling me that you can't get an hour
or two of the girl's time? And with all the money
I've got!

RICHARD It's too late now. In two days she's going to
Europe for two years. I'm going to see her alone
tomorrow evening for seven or eight minutes.

ANTHONY Seven or eight minutes!

RICHARD She's staying in the country at her aunt's.

ANTHONY Go and see her there!

RICHARD I can't. But I'm meeting her at the station with a
taxi tomorrow evening at 8.30. We'll drive to
Wallack's Theatre. She's meeting her mother and
some of her friends there.

ANTHONY *(Looking thoughtful)* It won't take long to
drive down Broadway to the theatre.

RICHARD I know. Will I get time to tell her everything
that I want to tell her? No. No, father, your
money can't help me. It can't buy me one minute
of time.

ANTHONY All right, Richard, my boy. Go out with your
friends now. You say that money can't buy time?
Well, money can buy most things.

True love is everything!

The same room, that evening. Anthony Rockwell is talking to his sister, Ellen. They are sitting in chairs. Ellen has a cup of coffee. Anthony has a glass of something stronger.

ANTHONY He says that ten million dollars can't buy a way into older and better families than ours, Ellen.

ELLEN Anthony, you're always thinking about money. But money is nothing. True love is everything! Why didn't Richard speak to the girl earlier?

ANTHONY I don't know.

ELLEN How could a girl say no to a fine boy like him? And now there's no time. When does she go to Europe?

ANTHONY The day after tomorrow.

'True love is everything!'

4

ELLEN   Poor Richard! All your money cannot make him
happy. Oh dear! Oh dear!

SCENE 3

The ring

*The same room, the next evening. Richard is dressed to
go out. Ellen is with him. She is giving him a ring.*

ELLEN   Wear this ring tonight. Your mother gave it to
me. She said that it brought good luck in love.
'Give it to Richard when he falls in love with a
girl,' she told me.

*Richard tries to put it on his smallest finger, but the ring
is too small. He puts it in his coat pocket.*

RICHARD   It's too small to wear, but I'll keep it safe.

ELLEN   Good luck, Richard.

RICHARD   Thank you, aunt.

SCENE 4

A lot of traffic

*Richard and Miss Lantry are in the back of a taxi. The
taxi driver is sitting in front.*

MISS LANTRY   We must hurry. Mother doesn't like waiting.

RICHARD *(To the taxi driver)* To Wallack's Theatre. As
quickly as you can, driver!

TAXI DRIVER Yes, sir. *(He starts driving.)*

RICHARD I want to tell you—

MISS LANTRY *(Looking out of the taxi)* Where are we?

RICHARD What? Oh, we're turning from Forty-Second
Street into Broadway. But I wanted to tell you—

MISS LANTRY How long will it take to get to the theatre?

RICHARD Seven or eight minutes. *(He takes the ring from
his pocket.)* I want to show you – oh! *(He drops
the ring and it falls out of the taxi window.)*
Driver, stop! Stop!

MISS LANTRY What is it?

RICHARD I've dropped a ring. It was my mother's. I must
look for it. I don't want to lose it. It won't take a
minute.

*Richard gets out of the taxi and looks on the ground.
Miss Lantry looks worriedly at her watch. The taxi
driver is looking round him in surprise. Traffic noises are
heard. After a minute, Richard comes back.*

RICHARD I've got it! On you go, driver.

TAXI DRIVER Sorry, sir. But I can't.

MISS LANTRY Why don't you drive on? We'll be late.

RICHARD *(Standing up in the taxi and looking round)* Has
all the traffic in New York stopped around us?
Where did it all come from?

6

'I've got it!'

TAXI DRIVER I don't know, sir.

MISS LANTRY Where are the police? Can't they help?

RICHARD I'm very sorry. We can't go on, and it'll take an
    hour to move all this traffic away!

MISS LANTRY Show me the ring. We can't help this.

    (*Smiling*) And I don't like theatres very much.

7

True love

Anthony Rockwell's bedroom. He is sitting up in bed reading. There is a knock at the door.

ANTHONY Who is it?

ELLEN It's me.

ANTHONY Come in, Ellen.

Ellen comes into the room. She looks excited.

ELLEN She is going to marry our Richard!

Anthony smiles. He does not look surprised.

ANTHONY Oh? Is that right?

Ellen sits down on a chair near the bed.

ELLEN They had to stop on the way to the theatre. And what stopped them? Not your money! It was a little ring!

ANTHONY (*Still smiling*) What happened? Tell me.

ELLEN Richard dropped the ring in the street. He got out to find it, and suddenly there was traffic everywhere!

ANTHONY How strange!

ELLEN Yes! It was two hours before the taxi could move again! So he had time to tell her that he loved her.

ANTHONY And they're going to marry, are they? Well, I'm happy to hear it.

8

ELLEN   Don't ever say 'Money can buy anything!' to me
again, Anthony. Not after tonight. It isn't true.
Money is nothing when you have true love.

SCENE 6

A good day's work

Next morning. Anthony is in his study. With him is Kelly.

ANTHONY   Thank you, Kelly. That was a good day's work.
Now, what did I give you? Five thousand dollars?
KELLY   Yes, Mr Rockwell, and I paid out three hundred
dollars of my own money. I got the taxis for five
dollars, but the other drivers wanted ten dollars.
But the police were the worst.
ANTHONY   Were they?
KELLY   Yes. They wanted fifty dollars. But everything
went beautifully, Mr Rockwell. Everybody arrived
at the right time. It was two hours before anybody
moved!
Rockwell gives Kelly a packet, with money inside it.
ANTHONY   Here you are, Kelly. One thousand for your
work, and your three hundred back. OK?
KELLY   Thank you.
ANTHONY   (*Laughing*) Thank *you*, Kelly. Money talks,
right?

INTRODUCTION

A young man's uncle leaves him one thousand dollars in his will. What can the young man do with it?

CHARACTERS IN THE PLAY

Bobby Gillian, a young man
Mr Tolman, a lawyer
Mr Sharp, a lawyer
Miss Hayden, a pretty young woman
Miss Lotta Lauriere, a dancer
Bryson, a man of forty
Man at the theatre

PERFORMANCE NOTES

Scene 1:   A lawyers' office, with a desk and two chairs
Scene 2:   A restaurant, with tables and chairs
Scene 3:   Theatre dressing room, with a dressing table, clothes cupboard and a mirror
Scene 4:   As Scene 1
Scene 5:   The living room in Bobby's uncle's house, with a table and chair
Scene 6:   As Scene 1

You will need a piece of paper that looks like a will, another piece of paper with writing on it, some writing paper, a pen, a packet of money, a book, and a cup.

One Thousand Dollars

The will

In Tolman and Sharp's office. Mr Tolman is sitting behind his desk. He has just finished reading a will. Bobby Gillian is sitting the other side of the desk.

TOLMAN Well, there you are. Your uncle wrote his will a month or two before he died, and now I've read it to you. What do you think?

BOBBY   (*Laughing*) It's not going to be easy to spend a thousand dollars. Fifty dollars or fifty thousand would be easier. I'll have to ask a friend how to spend it.

TOLMAN   Did you listen carefully when I was reading the will? After spending the thousand dollars, you must tell me, in writing, how you spent it. Will you do that?

BOBBY   Yes, I'll do it, Mr Tolman.

TOLMAN   (*Giving Bobby a packet*) Then here's the money. One thousand dollars.

SCENE 2

A lot or very little

At a restaurant. Bryson is sitting at a table, drinking coffee and reading a book. Bobby sits down opposite him.

BOBBY   Hello there, Bryson! Put down your book, I've got a funny story to tell you!

BRYSON   Tell it to somebody at one of the other tables. You know I don't like your stories.

BOBBY   It's a good story. I've just come from my uncle Septimus's lawyers. He's died and left me one thousand dollars! What can I do with it?

BRYSON   I thought old man Gillian had half a million.

'I've got a funny story to tell you!'

BOBBY   He did. He left most of it to the hospital that
killed him! Isn't that funny? His secretary gets ten
dollars, and I get a thousand.

BRYSON   You've always got plenty of money to spend.

BOBBY   Lots. Uncle Septimus was like Father Christmas
to me.

BRYSON   Did he have any other family?

BOBBY   None. There is a Miss Hayden who lives in his
house. She's a quiet little thing. The daughter of
one of my uncle's friends. I forgot to say that she
got ten dollars, too.

BRYSON   Did she?

13

BOBBY   Why didn't he leave me just ten dollars? Then I could spend it on two bottles of champagne and forget Uncle Septimus and his money.

BRYSON   (*Smiling*) A thousand dollars can be a lot or very little. One man could buy a happy home with it and laugh at America's richest man.

BOBBY   That's true.

BRYSON   A thousand dollars could buy milk for one hundred babies this summer, and save fifty of their lives. It could send a clever boy to college.

BOBBY   Listen, Bryson. I asked you to tell me what *I* could do with a thousand dollars.

BRYSON   (*Laughing*) Go and buy a gold necklace for your favourite dancer, Lotta Lauriere. Then go and work on a farm. Work with sheep. I've never liked sheep.

BOBBY   The beautiful Lotta! Yes, you're right. I want to spend all the money on one thing. You see, I've got to write and say what I spent it on, and I don't like writing. Thanks, Bryson!

SCENE 3
A necklace for Lotta

Lotta Lauriere's dressing room at the theatre. She is getting ready. There is a knock at the door.

14

'Who is it?'

LOTTA   Who is it?

BOBBY   It's me. Bobby Gillian.

LOTTA   Come in, Bobby. (*He comes in.*) What is it,
Bobby? I have to go and dance in two minutes.

BOBBY   Listen, Lotta. Would you like a pretty necklace? I
can spend a thousand. What do you say to that?

LOTTA   (*Laughing*) Oh, you sweet man! It's true that I
love pretty things. But . . .

BOBBY   Yes?

LOTTA   (*Putting on a hat*) Did you see the necklace that
Della Stacey was wearing the other night? It cost
more than two thousand dollars at Tiffany's.

BOBBY   Oh, did it?

There is a knock on the door. A man comes in.

MAN   Miss Lauriere, it's time!

LOTTA   Oh! I must go, Bobby!

Lotta leaves. The man waits for Bobby to leave.

BOBBY   What would *you* do with a thousand dollars?

MAN   Open a bar. I know a place that could make a lot
of money. Are you thinking of putting some
money into— ?

BOBBY   Oh, no. I only wanted to know.

MAN   Listen, this could make us both a lot of money.

BOBBY   Excuse me. I must go.

Bobby leaves the room.

MAN   And I thought it was my lucky day.

SCENE 4
Bobby asks a question

*In Tolman and Sharp's office. Tolman is sitting at his
desk. Bobby is standing the other side of Tolman's desk.
The lawyer does not look pleased to see him.*

TOLMAN What do you want now, Mr Gillian?

BOBBY Can I ask you a question? Did my uncle leave
Miss Hayden more than the ten dollars?

TOLMAN No, he didn't.

BOBBY Thank you very much, sir.

TOLMAN Is that all?

BOBBY Yes, thank you. That's all I wanted to know.

SCENE 5
News for Miss Hayden

*In Septimus Gillian's living room. Miss Hayden is sitting
at a table, writing letters. She looks up when Bobby
comes in.*

BOBBY I've just come from old Tolman's. They found a –
what's the word? – a codicil to the will.

MISS HAYDEN They did?

BOBBY Dear old uncle left you some more money. A

thousand dollars. Tolman asked me to bring it to you. Here it is. (*He puts the packet of money on the table.*)

MISS HAYDEN   Oh! Oh!

BOBBY   I love you, Miss Hayden. Did you know that?

MISS HAYDEN   Oh! No. I am sorry.

BOBBY   Is there no hope for me?

MISS HAYDEN   I – no, I am sorry.

BOBBY   (*Smiling*) Can I write a note?

MISS HAYDEN   Of course. (*She gives him a pen and some paper.*) I – please, excuse me.

She leaves. Bobby writes a short note, then reads it.

BOBBY   (*Reading*) 'Paid to the best and dearest woman in the world, one thousand dollars. For all the happiness she brings to people.'

SCENE 6
_____

Another fifty thousand!

In Tolman and Sharp's office. Tolman is sitting behind his desk when Bobby comes into the room.

BOBBY   I've spent the thousand dollars. And I've got a note to tell you what I spent it on.

He puts the note on Tolman's desk. Tolman gets up and goes to the door. He opens it.

'Is there no hope for me?'

TOLMAN   (*Calling*) Sharp! Come in here, please.

SHARP   (*Coming into the room*) Yes? (*He looks at Bobby, then looks down at the note.*) Oh. I understand.

He goes out of the room again. Tolman and Bobby wait silently. Sharp comes back with a piece of paper. The two lawyers read it and look at each other.

TOLMAN   Mr Gillian, there was a codicil to your uncle's will.

BOBBY   A codicil?

TOLMAN   We were told not to read it until you told us, in writing, how you spent the thousand dollars. You have now done this, so I will tell you what the codicil says.

BOBBY   Please do.

TOLMAN   Your uncle tells us in the codicil that we can give you another fifty thousand dollars—

BOBBY   (*Very surprised*) What!

TOLMAN   (*Continuing*) —if you have used the money to do some good for others. But . . .

BOBBY   But?

TOLMAN   If you have spent it carelessly or given it away to the wrong people—

BOBBY   (*Laughing*) As I usually do!

TOLMAN   Then the fifty thousand dollars must be paid to Miss Miriam Hayden. Now, Mr Gillian. Mr Sharp and I will read your note and find out—

20

Bobby quickly takes the note from the desk.

BOBBY (*Smiling*) It's all right. There's no need to read it.
I lost the thousand dollars betting on a horse at
the races. Goodbye, Mr Tolman, Mr Sharp.

He leaves the office, happily singing a song.

TOLMAN (*Laughing*) Are you surprised, Mr Sharp?

SHARP (*Shaking his head and smiling*) No, Mr Tolman.
Not surprised at all!

'Are you surprised, Mr Sharp?'

21

INTRODUCTION

Once every ten weeks, office worker Towers Chandler dresses like a man with a million dollars, goes to one of the best restaurants in New York, and eats the most expensive food. One evening, he meets a girl . . .

CHARACTERS IN THE PLAY

Towers Chandler, an office worker
Marian, a pretty young girl
Sissie, Marian's sister
Marie, a servant
Jeff White, an office worker
Mrs Black, whose house Chandler and White live in
Waiter
Four other people in the restaurant

PERFORMANCE NOTES

Scene 1: The doorway of a house
Scene 2: A street corner in New York
Scene 3: A restaurant, with three tables and six chairs, two chairs at each table
Scene 4: Marian's bedroom, with a bed, and other bedroom furniture

You will need coffee, cups, plates, some food and some wine for the other people in the restaurant.

A Night Out

One dollar a week

The doorway of the house where Chandler has a room.
He is dressed in his best clothes, ready for his evening
out. He is going out as his friend, Jeff White, comes in.

WHITE   What are you doing this evening, Towers?

CHANDLER   (*Smiling*) Tonight I'm going to live like a man
with a million dollars!

WHITE   What are you talking about? You haven't got a
million dollars!

CHANDLER   How much money are you and I paid each
week, Jeff?

WHITE   Eighteen dollars. Why?

CHANDLER   And how much of that eighteen dollars do you
spend each week?

WHITE   All of it, of course.

CHANDLER   Well, I don't. Each week I save one dollar out
of my eighteen. Then, every ten weeks, I can buy
myself an evening to remember.

WHITE   What do you do?

CHANDLER   I put on my finest clothes, go to one of the best
restaurants in New York, eat the most expensive

23

food on the menu, drink the best wine, then take a taxi home!

WHITE (*Very surprised*) Why?

CHANDLER Why? Because it makes me feel wonderful to sit with some of the richest people in America, and to make them think that I'm rich, too.

WHITE You're crazy!

CHANDLER (*Laughing*) Perhaps I am!

Mrs Black comes in.

MRS BLACK Ah, Mr Chandler. I wanted to see you.

CHANDLER Good evening, Mrs Black. What a lovely evening.

MRS BLACK Lovely evening perhaps, but you haven't paid me for your room this month. When am I going to get the money?

CHANDLER Soon, Mrs Black. Very soon.

Mrs Black looks at Chandler's clothes.

MRS BLACK You can spend money on expensive clothes, but you can't pay for your room. Is that right?

CHANDLER (*Hurrying away*) Goodnight, Mrs Black!

Scene 2

A pretty girl

A street in New York. Chandler is walking along the street when a girl, Marian, comes round the corner. She is wearing an old hat and a cheap-looking coat. She is moving quickly, walks into Chandler, and falls down.

MARIAN Oh!

CHANDLER Oh, dear!

Chandler helps her to get up. She has hurt her foot.

MARIAN My foot! I've hurt my foot.

CHANDLER Can you walk?

MARIAN I – I think I can.

She tries to walk, but her foot hurts too much.

MARIAN Oh! Perhaps—

CHANDLER I'll call a taxi to take you home.

MARIAN No, please. I'll be all right in a minute.

'Can you walk?'

Chandler looks at her carefully for the first time, and likes what he sees.

CHANDLER Your foot needs a longer rest, I think.

MARIAN Perhaps you're right.

CHANDLER I was on my way to eat by myself. Why don't you come with me? We'll have dinner together, and by then your foot will carry you home very nicely.

MARIAN But we don't know each other . . .

CHANDLER I'm Towers Chandler. Now that you know my name, come and have dinner. Then I'll say goodbye, or take you home if you prefer.

MARIAN But my clothes! They aren't—

CHANDLER I'm sure that you look prettier in them than anyone we shall see in the most expensive restaurant.

MARIAN Well . . . my foot does hurt. All right, Mr Chandler, I'll come. You can call me . . . Miss Marian.

SCENE 3
Chandler tells a story

Chandler and Marian are sitting at a restaurant table. A waiter is giving them coffee. There are two other tables near them. The people sitting at them are dressed expensively and are talking quietly while eating.

MARIAN That was a very good dinner. Thank you, Mr
Chandler. Tell me, what do you do?

CHANDLER (*Laughing*) Do? I ride my horses, go dancing,
travel to Europe. And then there's my boat.

MARIAN Haven't you got any work to do? Something
more – well, interesting?

CHANDLER My dear Miss Marian, there's no time for
work! Think of dressing every day for dinner, and
of calling at the houses of six or seven friends
every afternoon or evening.

MARIAN Yes – well—

CHANDLER Oh yes, we 'do-nothings' are the hardest
workers in the country!

MARIAN (*Sadly*) I see. Well, thank you for a nice time. I
must go home now. My foot is much better. I can
walk home. There's no need for you to come with
me.

CHANDLER Oh. Well, goodbye, Miss Marian.

*She gets up from the table and walks away. Chandler
watches her, sadly.*

CHANDLER (*Talking to himself*) What a wonderful girl! A
shop girl, perhaps? Why didn't I tell her the true
story of my life? Perhaps then . . . well, it's too
late now. Oh, how stupid I am!

The right man for Marian

In Marian's bedroom. She is with her sister, Sissie. Both girls are sitting on the bed, talking excitedly.

SISSIE It's two hours since you ran out in that old coat and hat. Mother has been very worried. She sent Louis in the car to find you. You *are* a bad girl!

Marie comes into the room.

SISSIE Ah, there you are, Marie. Tell mother that Miss Marian is home again.

MARIE Yes, miss. (*She leaves the room.*)

MARIAN I only ran down to my dressmaker's to tell her to use blue on my new dress instead of red. Marie's old hat and coat were just what I needed.

SISSIE You're crazy!

MARIAN (*Laughing*) Everyone thought that I was a shop girl! It was wonderful!

SISSIE Dinner is finished. You're very late.

MARIAN I know. I fell and hurt my foot. I couldn't walk, so I went to a restaurant and sat there until I was better. (*She gets up from the bed and walks to the window. She looks down into the street below.*) We'll have to marry one day, Sissie.

SISSIE Yes, that's true.

'I could love a man with kind blue eyes.'

MARIAN   We're rich, and mother and father will want us
to marry somebody who is as rich as we are. But
can I *love* a man like that?

SISSIE   Who could you love?

MARIAN   I could love a man with kind blue eyes, who
doesn't try to make love to every girl he sees. But
I could only love him if he has some important
work to do in the world. Then it doesn't matter
how poor he is.

SISSIE   You *are* crazy!

MARIAN   Perhaps. But, sister dear, we only meet men who
ride their horses and go dancing. I couldn't love a
man like that, even if his eyes are blue and he's
kind to poor girls who meet him in the street.

INTRODUCTION

Who is the man who comes into Miss Martha's shop? Why does he buy two loaves of stale bread each time he comes? Miss Martha is very interested in him.

CHARACTERS IN THE PLAY

Miss Martha, a woman who sells bread and cakes in her shop
Blumberger, a man who comes into the shop for bread
Kelton, a man who works with Blumberger
Mrs Annie Green, Miss Martha's friend
Mrs Green's friend, a woman
A man in the shop
A woman in the shop

PERFORMANCE NOTES

Each of the four scenes happens in the shop. You will need four loaves of bread, some cakes, two packets of butter, a knife to cut bread, a painting, and some paper bags.

Two Loaves of Bread

The man who buys stale bread

Inside the baker's shop. Miss Martha is standing behind the counter, talking to her friend, Mrs Annie Green.

MISS MARTHA He comes in two or three times a week, and he always buys two loaves of stale bread.

MRS GREEN *Stale* bread?

MISS MARTHA Always stale bread, never fresh bread. Of course, fresh bread is five cents a loaf, stale bread is five cents for *two* loaves.

MRS GREEN And you think he's poor?

MISS MARTHA Oh, yes, he is, Annie, I'm sure. One day I saw some red and brown paint on his fingers. 'He's a painter,' I said to myself.

MRS GREEN Well, we all know that painters are very often poor. But can you be sure that he's a painter? Just because he has paint on his fingers . . .

Miss Martha takes a painting out from under the counter.

MISS MARTHA I'm going to put this on my wall. If he's a painter, he'll see it and say something about it.

MRS GREEN (*Laughing*) Very clever, Martha. But tell me, are you a little in love with this man?

MISS MARTHA   Annie! (*Laughing*) Well, perhaps a little.

The painting on the wall

In the shop, the next day. The painting is now on the
wall behind the counter. Miss Martha is putting some
bread and some cakes into a man's bag. He gives her
some money, then goes out of the shop. Mr Blumberger
comes into the shop. His clothes are poor but tidy.

BLUMBERGER   Good morning. Two loaves of stale bread,
        please.
MISS MARTHA   (*Smiling*) Good morning.
She puts two loaves of bread into paper bags. While she
is doing this, Blumberger is looking at the picture on the
wall.
BLUMBERGER   That is a fine picture.
MISS MARTHA   Is it? I do love . . . paintings. Is this a good
        picture, do you think?
BLUMBERGER   The colour's good but the lines are not right.
        Good morning.
He takes the bread and leaves the shop. As he leaves,
Mrs Green enters with a friend.
MRS GREEN   (*Excited*) Is that him?
MISS MARTHA   Yes!

MRS GREEN   (*To her friend*) That's the man! You know, I
    was telling you about him. (*To Miss Martha*) Did
    he see the painting?

MISS MARTHA   Yes! He knew at once that it was a good
    painting. Oh, what kind eyes he's got!

FRIEND   And he only eats stale bread?

MISS MARTHA   Yes. He must be very poor. And he looks so
    thin. Oh, I do want to help him.

MRS GREEN   (*Laughing*) You want to marry him!

FRIEND   Where does he
    live?

MISS MARTHA   I don't know.
    Some poor room
    somewhere. But if
    we marry . . .

MRS GREEN   He can come
    and live here, with
    you, over the shop!
    Stop dreaming,
    Martha!

FRIEND   What's wrong
    with dreaming?
    Sometimes dreams
    come true.

MISS MARTHA   That's right!
    They do!

'But if we marry . . .'

33

Miss Martha tries to help

Two days later. A man and a woman are in the shop.
The woman is looking at the cakes, trying to decide
what to have. Miss Martha is putting some butter into a
bag for the man. She is now wearing her best clothes,
and her hair looks different.

WOMAN   Now, what shall I have?

MAN   (*To Miss Martha*) Thank you. Good morning.
He leaves the shop with the bag.

MISS MARTHA   (*To the woman*) Have you decided?

WOMAN   No, I—
She stops speaking as Blumberger comes into the shop.

MISS MARTHA   (*To Blumberger*) Good morning.

BLUMBERGER   Good morning. Two stale loaves, please.

MISS MARTHA   (*Smiling*) How are you today?

BLUMBERGER   I'm very well—
We hear an ambulance going past outside. Blumberger
and the woman both go to the shop door to look out.
Miss Martha quickly cuts into each of the stale loaves,
and puts some butter in them. She puts the loaves into
paper bags. Blumberger and the woman come back to
the counter. Blumberger pays Miss Martha. The woman
goes back to look at the cakes.

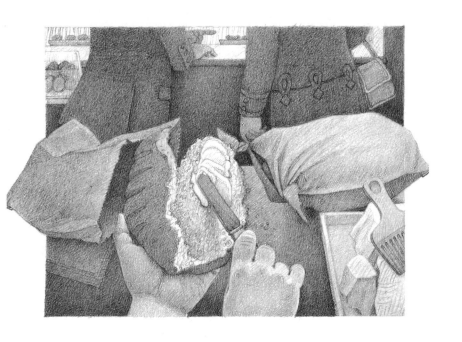

BLUMBERGER Thank you. Goodbye.

MISS MARTHA Goodbye.

WOMAN Now, what cakes shall I buy?

SCENE 4
A terrible mistake

Later that day. Miss Martha is in the shop with Mrs Green.

MRS GREEN So what did you do?

MISS MARTHA I put some butter in the bread! He didn't see
me, of course. He was busy watching the
ambulance. I had to be very quick.

MRS GREEN   How kind you are, Martha.

MISS MARTHA   I can't let him eat only stale bread, Annie.
He needs some good food, poor man.

MRS GREEN   What will he say when he sees the butter?
He'll know it was you who put it there.

MISS MARTHA   (*Smiling*) Yes, he will. (*She suddenly looks worried.*) Do you think that he'll be angry?

MRS GREEN   No, of course not. Not if he's hungry. But I must go. I'll see you tomorrow, Martha.

MISS MARTHA   Goodbye, Annie.

Mrs Green leaves the shop. Martha begins moving one or two things, making the shop tidy. Then she sits down behind the counter and starts to read a book. Suddenly the door opens, and Blumberger and Kelton come in. Blumberger is angry, but Kelton is trying to hold him back.

BLUMBERGER   (*Shouting at Martha*) You stupid woman!

KELTON   Wait! Blumberger!

BLUMBERGER   You stupid, stupid woman! Do you know what you've done? You've ruined my work!

KELTON   Come on! You've said enough! It was an accident, I'm sure.

Kelton pulls Blumberger out of the shop. After a minute, Kelton comes back again.

MISS MARTHA   What's wrong with him?

KELTON   That's Blumberger. He's an architect. We work together, in the same office.

36

'You've ruined my work!'

MISS MARTHA But what did I do wrong?

KELTON He's worked hard for three months now, on a
　　　　plan for the new city hospital. It was a
　　　　competition, and Blumberger was sure that he
　　　　was going to win it.

MISS MARTHA But . . . why— ?

KELTON I'm telling you, miss. You see, he finished putting
　　　　in the ink lines yesterday. When it's finished, he
　　　　always rubs out the pencil lines with stale bread.

MISS MARTHA So that's why he wanted the stale bread!

KELTON Well, today – well, you know, that butter got
　　　　right into the bread and when he tried to rub out
　　　　the pencil lines – well, Blumberger's plan is
　　　　ruined now, miss.

*Kelton turns and leaves the shop. Miss Martha puts her
head into her hands and starts to cry.*

EXERCISES

A Checking your understanding

All that Money can Buy

1 *How much can you remember? Check your answers.*
   1 How much does Richard pay for his suits?
   2 Why did Richard's mother want him to have the ring?
   3 How much did Kelly have to pay the police?

One Thousand Dollars

2 *Who in this play . . .*
   1 . . . left Bobby one thousand dollars?
   2 . . . is Bobby's favourite dancer?
   3 . . . does Bobby think is 'the dearest woman in the world'?

A Night Out

3 *Choose the best question-word and answer these questions.*
   why   how   where
   1 . . . much does Chandler save each week?
   2 . . . does Chandler take Marian?
   3 . . . couldn't Marian love a man like Chandler?

Two Loaves of Bread

4 *Who said these words in this play?*
   1 'But can you be sure that he's a painter?'
   2 'The colour's good but the lines are not right.'
   3 'I put some butter in the bread!'
   4 'When it's finished, he always rubs out the pencil lines
     with stale bread.'

B Working with language

One Thousand Dollars

1 *Complete these sentences with information from the play.*
   1 Bobby's Uncle Septimus had . . . dollars, but he left most
     of it to . . . that . . . him!
   2 Lotta's friend, . . . , was wearing . . . that cost . . .
   3 Tolman could not read the codicil to the will until . . .
   4 Bobby tells Tolman that he lost the thousand dollars by . . .

All that Money can Buy

2 *Put together these beginnings and endings of sentences.*
   1 a way into older and better families.
   2 to take you to the Bahamas in two days.
   3 your money can't buy me
   4 how could a girl say no
   5 I can have a boat ready
   6 to a fine boy like him?

C Activities

1 You are Anthony Rockwell. Richard has just told you
   about his love for Miss Lantry. You have asked Kelly to
   come to see you. Write your conversation with Kelly as you
   explain what you want him to do.

2 Anthony Rockwell says, 'Money talks, right?' He thinks
   that money can buy anything. Do you agree or disagree?
   Write your answer, giving your reasons.

3 What would you spend a thousand dollars on? Discuss this
   with your friends, and write down all your ideas.

D Project work

One hundred years ago, fresh bread cost five cents a loaf in
New York. Can you find out how much it costs today? And
what about in your country? How much is a loaf of bread
today, and how much did it cost a hundred years ago?
Make a list of some different kinds of food and find out
about prices now and in the past.

GLOSSARY

architect someone whose job is to plan new buildings

aunt your father's or mother's sister

bar a place where you can buy and drink alcohol

bet (in this play) to pay money, saying which horse will
win a race. If your horse wins, you win; if it loses, you
lose

butter soft yellow food that is made from milk

champagne an expensive French wine with bubbles in it

codicil something written after a will is already made,
which gives more instructions about the money

competition a test in which people try to do better than
each other

counter a kind of narrow table in a shop where you go to
pay for something you buy

crazy mad, stupid

dream (in this play) to hope for something good in the
future

fresh (of food) recently made and good to eat

ink coloured liquid used for writing, and sometimes for
making pictures or plans

lawyer someone whose job is to help people with the law

line a long thin mark put on paper with a pen or pencil

loaf (plural **loaves**) a big piece of bread

necklace something pretty (and often expensive) that you wear round your neck

paint (*n*) coloured liquid used to make pictures

paint (*v*) to make a picture with paints

painting a picture

pretty beautiful, nice to look at

race (in this play) a competition to see which horse can run the fastest

rub out to take off something that is written on paper

ruin to spoil or damage something so that it is no longer any good

servant someone who works (for example, cooking or cleaning) in another person's house

sir a polite way to speak to a man who is more important than you

stale old and dry, not fresh

waiter somebody who brings your food or drink in a restaurant

will a piece of paper that says who will have your money, house and other things when you die

wine a strong drink made of grapes